The Wonde

Book of Dad Jokes

500+ Cheesy, terrible, cringy, head in hands one-liners and puns that are so bad they are good, a great gift for new fathers, become a hilarious funny Dad

---

JOHN NERO

Dedication

I would like to dedicate this book to my Dad and my Brother, without a doubt two of the best Dad's out there, and both of them are full to the brim with horrendous jokes!

Thank you for always making me laugh, lets share a bit of that with everyone else 😔

What is a "Dad Joke"

In my humble opinion a dad joke has to satisfy the following criteria

- Inoffensive (no swear words)
- Fairly short
- Very corny
- As likely to receive a groan as it is a laugh

Dad jokes are always made with the intention of making someone smile, and once you become a father you need to be armed with jokes suitable for all ages. But for some reason no matter how bad they get we just can't stop telling them!

I hope this collection puts a smile on your face 😊

JOHN NERO

For a range of parenting books, guides
and gift ideas please search John Nero on
Amazon or visit my website.

www.johnnero.com

SCAN ME

#1

I'm afraid for the calendar. Its days are numbered.

#2

I had a long conversation with a dolphin once. We just seemed to click.

#3

I've got a pen that can write underwater. It can write other words too but underwater is one of my faves.

#4

My son put his shoes on the wrong feet. I don't even know where he got someone else's feet.

#5

I don't want to brag but I made six figures last year. I was named worst employee at the toy factory.

#6

What's the difference between a hippo and a Zippo? One is very heavy, the other is a little lighter.

#7

I bought some shoes from a drug dealer. I don't know what he laced them with, but I was tripping all day!

#8

I failed my driving test when the instructor asked me, "What do you do at a red light?" I said, "I usually check Facebook."

#9

What kind of egg did the evil chicken lay? A deviled egg.

#10

I smeared some ketchup all over my eyes. It was a bad idea in Heinz-sight.

#11

What do you call a bear with no teeth? A gummy bear!

#12

The rotation of earth really makes my day.

#13

A slice of apple pie is $2.50 in Jamaica and $3.00 in the Bahamas. These are the pie rates of the Caribbean.

#14
Have you ever tried to catch fog? I tried yesterday but I mist.

#15
What do you call a line of men waiting to get their haircut? A barberqueue.

#16
At first, I thought my chiropractor wasn't any good, but now I stand corrected.

#17
What do you call a man who can't stand? Neil.

#18
My printer's name is Bob Marley. Because it's always jammin'.

#19

I'm going to take up meditation. I figure it's better than sitting around doing nothing.

#20

Why was the ghost so tired? He worked the graveyard shift.

#21

Why couldn't the bicycle stand up on its own? It was two tired.

#22

I told my wife she drew her eyebrows too high. She seemed surprised!

#23

Two aerials meet on a roof, fall in love, and get married. The wedding was rubbish, but the reception was brilliant

#24

Where do Dads keep their Dad jokes? In the Dad-a-base.

#25

I made a belt made of watches? It was a waist of time.

#26

To the thief that stole my copy of Microsoft Office, I will track you down. You have my Word.

#27

Does anyone need an ark? I Noah guy.

#28

Why did the old man fall into the well? Because he couldn't see that well!

#29

Last year, I wrote a book on penguins. In retrospect, paper would have been easier.

#30

Did you know humans eat more bananas than monkeys? It's true. When was the last time you ate a monkey?

#31

What's a guitar teacher's favorite Italian food? Strum-boli.

#32

How does a rancher keep track of his cattle? With a cow-culator.

#33

Knives will never go obsolete. They're cutting edge technology.

#34

What do you call an unpredictable camera? A loose Canon.

#35

What do you call a priest who becomes a lawyer? A father-in-law.

#36

Two goldfish are in a tank. One says, "Do you know how to drive this thing?"

#37

I used to really hate facial hair, but then it grew on me.

#38

Everyone knows Murphy's Law: anything that can go wrong will go wrong. But have you heard of Cole's Law? It's thinly sliced cabbage.

#39

Our dog used to chase people on a scooter. It got so bad we had to take his scooter away.

#40

I was feeling nostalgic so I put the car in reverse, it really took me back.

#41

Why don't crabs give to charity?
Because they are shellfish!

#42

I really like telling Dad jokes.
Sometimes he even laughs!

#43

What do you call a can opener that
doesn't work? A can't opener!

#44

Why was Cinderella thrown off the
basketball team? She ran away from
the ball.

#45

What do clouds wear under their
clothes? Thunderwear.

#46
Why did the picture go to prison?
Because it was framed

#47
Do I enjoy making courthouse puns?
Guilty.

#48
As I handed my Dad his 50th birthday card, he said. "You know, one would have been enough."

#49
Why don't astronomers like Orion's Belt? It's a big waist of space.

#50
I saw an ad that read: "TV for sale, $1, volume stuck on full." I thought to myself, "I can't turn that down!"

#51

What do you call cheese that doesn't belong to you? Nacho cheese.

#52

I went to the doctor because I can see into the future. The doctor asked how long I have suffered from this? I said, "Since next Monday."

#53

I worked in a shoe-recycling shop. It was sole destroying!

#54

Why are skeletons so calm? Because nothing gets under their skin.

#55

The early bird catches the worm,
I'll sleep in until there are pancakes
thanks!

#56

Over a century ago, two brothers
thought it was possible to fly. And
as you can see, they were Wright.

#57

I tried to explain to my 4-year-old
son that it's ok to accidentally poop
your pants. But he's still making fun
of me.

#58

Why did the computer get mad at
the printer? Because it didn't like
its toner voice.

#59

What does garlic do if it gets too hot? It takes its cloves off.

#60

What's the best thing about having a party at a haunted house? The ghosts have loads of boos.

#61

What did the sea say to the beach? Nothing, it just waved.

#62

How many apples grow on a tree? All of them!

#63

A cheese factory exploded, Da brie is everywhere!

#64
After dinner, my wife asked if I could clear the table. I needed a running start, but I made it!

#65
They have just opened the first restaurant on the moon! It's got great food but no atmosphere.

#66
What has four wheels and flies? A garbage truck.

#67
Why do you never see elephants hiding in trees? Because they're so good at it!

#68

I was convinced the dryer was shrinking my clothes. It turns out it was the refrigerator all along.

#69

I had to close down my dating service for chickens. I was struggling to make hens meet.

#70

How did Darth Vader know what Luke got him for Christmas? He felt his presents!

#71

Where do polar bears keep their money? The snow bank.

#72

I was recently told I was going deaf. The news was hard for me to hear.

#73
Did you hear about the Yacht builder that had to work from home? His sails went through the roof.

#74
Why can't a toe be 12 inches long? Because then it would be a foot.

#75
Swimming with sharks is really expensive, it cost me an arm and a leg.

#76
I accidentally took my cat's tablets last night, don't ask meow!

#77

My boss asked me why I only seem to get sick on weekdays? I told him I have a weekend immune system.

#78

I don't trust atoms. They make up everything!

#79

Where do math teachers go on holiday? Times Square.

#80

Why can't you eat Wookie meat? Because it's too chewy.

#81

What has four fingers and a thumb and isn't your hand? My hand.

#82
Why did the poor man stock up on yeast? To make some dough.

#83
Why are ghosts, such bad liars? You can see right through them.

#84
How did the dog stop the music? Paws.

#85
I work in a factory that makes okay products. It's a satisfactory job.

#86
What did the Dad buffalo say when he dropped his son off at school? Bison.

#87

I decided to go visit my childhood home. I knocked on the door and asked if I could have a look inside because I was feeling nostalgic, they said no and slammed the door in my face. My parents are the worst.

#88

What has more letters than the alphabet? The post office!

#89

I went to the zoo and saw a baguette in a cage. The zookeeper said it was bread in captivity.

#90

What rhymes with orange? No it doesn't!

#91
Do you know how to make 7 even?
Take away the s.

#92
I thought about going on an all-almond die, but that's just nuts!

#93
Why is Dark spelled with a 'K' and not a 'C'? Because you can't 'C' in the dark

#94
Which is faster, hot or cold? Hot, because you can catch a cold.

#95
I was addicted to soap, but I'm clean now.

#96
What's the definition of surprise? A fart with a lump in it.

#97
Do you know how a penguin builds its house? Igloos it together.

#98
I have a joke about a broken clock, but it's not the right time.

#99
I wanted to go on a diet, but I feel like I have way too much on my plate right now.

#100
Last time I went on holiday I got charged extra for air conditioning. That wasn't cool.

#101

Sundays are always a little sad, but the day before is a sadder day.

#102

If two vegans get in an argument, is it still called a beef?

#103

What did one hat say to the other? Stay here! I'm going on ahead.

#104

Why was the horse so happy? Because he lived in a stable environment.

#105

How do you organize a space party? You planet.

#106
What does a house wear? Address!

#107
Why is cold water so insecure?
Because no one ever says it's hot.

#108
I tell you what, mountains aren't
just funny. They're hill areas.

#109
What does the dentist of the year
get? A little plaque.

#110
Why are pigs bad at sports? They
always hog the ball.

#111
How can you tell if a tree is
dogwood? By its bark.

#112
You can't trust stairs. They're always up to something.

#113
I sat down in a restaurant, the waiter asked, "Do you want to hear today's special?" I said, "Yes please." Waiter: "No problem, sir. Today is special."

#114
Where do sharks go on vacation? Finland.

#115
What do you call an elephant that doesn't matter? An irrelephant.

#116
What do bees use to brush their hair? A honeycomb!

#117

My wife suggested I should do lunges to stay in shape. I think that would be a big step forward.

#118

I have a joke about procrastination, but I'll tell it to you later.

#119

Bigfoot is sometimes confused for Sasquatch — Yeti never complains.

#120

What is the tallest building in the world? The library, it's got the most stories.

#121

Can February March? No, but April May!

#122

How do you make holy water? You boil the hell out of it.

#123

What did the big flower say to the little flower? "Hey there, bud."

#124

My aunt's astrological sign was cancer, funny considering how she died. She was killed by a giant crab

#125

Why couldn't the skeleton climb the mountain? He didn't have the guts.

#126

Ladies, if he can't appreciate your fruit puns. you need to let that mango.

#127
I just watched a program about beavers. It was the best dam program I've ever seen.

#128
Where do pirates buy their hooks? Second hand stores.

#129
Did you hear about the girl who quit her job at the doughnut factory? She was fed up with the hole business.

#130
What do you call a cow with no legs? Ground beef!

#131
Why couldn't the mail person deliver any envelopes? They were stationary.

#132
Why are frogs so happy? They eat whatever bugs them.

#133
My wife said I was being immature. I told her to get out of my fort.

#134
What did Baby Corn say to Mummy Corn? "Where's Pop Corn?"

#135
What do you call a hippie's wife? Mississippi.

#136
The last thing my grandfather said to me before he kicked the bucket was watch how far I can kick this bucket.

#137
Towels tell pretty good jokes, but they have a dry sense of humor.

#138
If I ever find the surgeon that messed up my limb replacement surgery, I'll kill him with my bear hands.

#139
Dad, can you please put my shoes on? No, they won't fit me.

#140
A steak pun is a rare medium well done.

#141
People say they pick their nose, but I was just born with mine.

#142
An apple a day keeps the doctor away if you throw it hard enough.

#143
There was a kidnapping at the school yesterday. It's okay, he woke up.

#144
I can't believe I got fired from the calendar factory. All I did was take a day off.

#145

What did the proton say to the electron? Stop being so negative all the time!

#146

My Dad's sister never comes to any group gatherings, she is my socially dist-aunt

#147

I was a personal trainer. Then got my too weak notice.

#148

I recently bumped into the guy that sold me an antique globe. It's a small world.

#149

I asked my cat what's three minus three. He said nothing.

#150
Did you hear about the burger that couldn't stop telling jokes? It was on a roll.

#151
What has one horn and gives milk? A milk truck.

#152
There are a lot of jokes about retired people, but none of them work!

#153
An invisible man married an invisible woman. The kids were nothing to look at.

#154
What do you get when you cross fish and an elephant? Swimming trunks.

#155

I'm going to have a go at attaching a light to the ceiling, but I'm afraid I'll probably screw it up.

#156

I recently decided to take up fencing. The neighbors said they will call the police unless I put it back.

#157

Do you know the best thing about living in Switzerland? Neither do I, but the flag is a big plus.

#158

What did the fisherman say to the magician? Pick a cod, any cod.

#159

We're renovating the house, and the first floor is going great, but the second floor is another story.

#160

Many people think Thor's brother is intense, but I found him to be low-key.

#161

RIP boiling water, you will be mist.

#162

While playing chess with my friend and he said, "Let's make this interesting." So we stopped playing chess.

#163

I was really angry at Mark for stealing my dictionary. I said, "Mark, my words!"

#164

I got fired from an orange juice company. Apparently, I couldn't concentrate.

#165

What do you call a fly without wings? A walk.

#166

I don't buy anything with velcro. It's a total rip-off.

#167

What do you call it when Batman skips church? Christian Bale.

#168
How do you deal with a fear of speed bumps? You slowly get over it.

#169
Dogs can't operate MRI machines. But catscan.

#170
What's orange and sounds like a parrot? A carrot!

#171
How do you lift an elephant with one hand? You can't, elephant only have feet.

#172
Did you hear the rumor about the butter? Well, I'm not going to spread it!

#173

Have you heard about the new movie constipation? It never came out.

#174

What do you call a sleeping bull? A bulldozer.

#175

Did you hear about the scientist whose lab partners with a pot of boiling water? He had a very esteemed colleague.

#176

Why is it a bad idea to iron a four-leaf clover? Because you shouldn't press your luck

#177
I didn't want to believe that my Dad was stealing from his job working on the roads, but I got home an all the signs were there.

#178
Where do you learn to make a banana split? In sundae school.

#179
Why wouldn't the sesame seed leave the casino? He was on a roll.

#180
Every night, I stay up trying to remember something, then it dawns on me.

#181
The difference between a numerator and a denominator is a short line. Only a fraction of people will understand this

#182
Why do cows have hooves and not feet? They lactose.

#183
My dog has no nose. How does it smell? Awful!

#184
What did the policeman say to his belly button? You're under a vest!

#185
Where do trees go to learn? Elementree school.

#186
I just started a seafood diet. I see food and I eat it.

#187
Someone has glued my pack of cards together. I don't know how to deal with it.

#188
How do celebrities stay cool? They have lots of fans.

#189
Elevator jokes are great, they work on many levels.

#190
When a child refuses to nap, are they guilty of resisting a rest?

#191
Why is 2019 afraid of 2020?
Because they had a fight and 2021.

#192
There's a new type of broom in stores. It's sweeping the nation!

#193
Why can't leopards hide? Because they are always spotted.

#194
I have a joke about being an electrician, but it's too shocking.

#195
What did the grape do when he got stepped on? He let out a little whine.

#196

People are making apocalypse jokes like there is no tomorrow!

#197

When is a car not a car? When it turns into a driveway!

#198

Five out of four people admit they're bad with fractions!

#199

What did one wall say to the other? I'll meet you at the corner.

#200

A Vicks VapoRub truck overturned on road this morning. There was no congestion for eight hours!

#201
What is heavy forward but not backward? A ton.

#202
Why do golfers carry an extra pair of socks? In case they get a hole in one!

#203
Why do scuba divers fall backwards into the water? If they fell forward they'd still be in the boat.

#204
What's an astronaut's favorite part of a keyboard? The Space Bar.

#205
How did the barber win the race? He knew a shortcut.

#206

After a bad harvest, why did the farmer start his own music label? Because he had a ton of sick beets.

#207

What does a zombie vegetarian eat? "GRRRAAAIINS!"

#208

What's ET short for? Because he's only got little legs!

#209

Which school subject was the witch's favorite? Spelling.

#210

A burger walks into a bar with a hotdog. The bartender says, "Sorry, we don't serve food here."

#211
What do Santa's elves listen to at the north pole? Wrap music!

#212
You should never date a tennis player. Love means nothing to them.

#213
How many tickles does it take to make an octopus laugh? Ten tickles.

#214
"Dad, can you please explain to me what a solar eclipse is?" No sun.

#215
Why is Peter Pan always flying? He neverlands.

#216
Why do ducks have tail feathers?
To cover their buttquacks.

#217
Three conspiracy theorists walk into
a bar. That can't just be a
coincidence.

#218
Why did the banana cross the road?
To get to the doctor's, he wasn't
peeling very well.

#219
What do you call a beehive with no
exit? Unbelievable.

#220

I just watched all the Harry Potter movies back to back with a friend. It wasn't the best idea, I couldn't see the TV.

#221

A ship carrying red paint crashed into a ship carrying blue in the middle of the ocean. Both crews were marooned.

#222

Do you know what the strongest days are? Saturday and Sunday. The rest are weekdays.

#223

A pun is not completely matured until it is full groan

#224

What's Forrest Gump's computer password? 1forrest1.

#225

What kind of tea do you drink with the queen? Royal-tea.

#226

What did one eye say to the other eye? "Between you and me, something smells."

#227

I asked the guy in the computer shop "How do you make a Motherboard?" He said, "I tell her about my job."

#228

What do you call a donkey with three legs? A wonkey!

#229

How do flat-earthers travel? On a plane.

#230

How much does Santa pay to park his sleigh? Nothing, it's on the house.

#231

What is the best Christmas present ever? A broken drum, you can't beat it!

#232

A police officer caught two kids playing with a firework and a car battery. He charged one and let the other off.

#233

What do a tick and the Eiffel Tower have in common? They're both Paris sites.

#234

I got my best friend a fridge for his birthday. I can't wait to see his face light up when he opens it!

#235

I was going to tell you a time-traveling joke, but you didn't like it.

#236

I wanted to start a professional hide and seek team, but unfortunately, it didn't work out. Good players are hard to find.

#237

The only thing flat-earthers fear is sphere itself

#238

What happens when frogs don't pay their parking tickets? They get toad.

#239

Dad, I'm hungry, Hi Hungry, I'm Dad.

#240

What do you call a sad cup of coffee? A Depresso.

#241

I have a joke about drilling, but it's boring.

#242

Did you hear the joke about the roof? Never mind, it's over your head.

#243

What do you call a group of killer whales playing instruments? An Orca-stra!

#244

I don't really like funerals that start before noon. I guess I'm just not a mourning person!

#245

Why was the burglar so sensitive? He takes things personally.

#246

Why can't eggs tell jokes? They'd crack each other up.

#247
What do you call an alligator detective? An investi-gator.

#248
I gave away all my used batteries today. Free of charge!

#249
I had a dream I weighed less than a thousandth of a gram. I was like, Omg.

#250
Did you hear the story about the haunted lift? It really raised my spirits!

#251
I bought a pencil with two erasers. It was pointless.

#252
Why doesn't a photon have any luggage? It's traveling light.

#253
When is a door not a door? When it's ajar.

#254
Why is the grass so dangerous? It's full of blades.

#255
What do frogs wear on their feet in summer? Open toad sandals

#256
I have a joke about statistics, but it's not significant.

#257

I defeated a chess champion in five moves. Finally, my high school karate lessons paid off

#258

What did the mountain climber name his son? Cliff

#259

What did the drummer call his twin daughters? Anna one, Anna two.

#260

How do lawyers say goodbye? Sue you soon!

#261

I recently quit my job as a butler. I refuse to be ordered around in that manor.

#262

What do you call a pile of cats? A meow-tain.

#263

What's red and smells like blue paint? Red paint.

#264

Why do vampires seem ill? They're always coffin.

#265

Which day do chickens hate the most? Friday.

#266

Why did the coffee call the police? It was mugged.

#267

Why couldn't the sailor learn his alphabet? He kept getting lost at C.

#268

Why do dogs float? Because they are good buoys.

#269

I'll call you later. Don't call me later, call me Dad!

#270

I once wrote a song about a tortilla, but it's more of a wrap.

#271

I just watched a fascinating documentary about how the Empire State Building was built. It was riveting!

#272

My Dad always went the extra mile for me. That's why I call him father

#273

It's not appropriate to make a 'Dad joke' if you're not a Dad. It's a faux pa.

#274

What do you get when you cross a snowman and a vampire? Frost bite.

#275

A rancher had only had 48 cows on his property, but when he rounded them up he had 50.

#276

What does a lemon say when it picks up the phone? "Yellow!"

#277
I've got a great joke about nepotism. But I'll only tell it to my kids.

#278
I thought of a great joke about construction, but I'm still working on it.

#279
What did the banana say to the boy? Nothing, bananas can't talk!

#280
What side of a tree grows the most branches? The outside!

#281
Why are pediatricians always so angry? Because they have little patients.

#282
What do you call a baby monkey? A chimp off the old block.

#283
I'm really looking forward to this year's Fibonacci convention. It's going to be as big as the last two put together.

#284
My wife said I ruined her birthday. Impossible, I didn't even KNOW it was her birthday!

#285
What's the fastest liquid on earth? Milk, It's pasteurized before you even see it.

#286
What do you call a dinosaur with an extensive vocabulary? A thesaurus.

#287
I'm that good at sleeping, I can do it with my eyes closed!

#288
What do you call a burger on wheels? Fast food!

#289
Two guys walked into a bar. The third guy ducked.

#290
Did I ever tell you about the time I use to be in a Jamaican band? No major part I played the triangle. I use to stand in the back and ting

#291

Why are balloons so expensive?
Inflation.

#292

What kind of music do planets like?
Neptunes.

#293

What did the shy pebble wish for?
That he was a little boulder.

#294

Why did the cookie go to the
doctor's office? He was feeling
crummy

#295

My cat was just sick on the carpet. I
don't think he's feline well.

#296
Why do geologists hate their jobs?
They get taken for granite.

#297
I once fell in love while doing a
forwards roll, I was head over heels!

#298
Lance isn't a very common name
these days, but in medieval times,
they were called lance-a-lot.

#299
You can't run through a campsite.
You can only ran, because it's past
tents.

#300
What kind of drink can be bitter
and sweet? Reali-tea.

#301

Although I can play piano by ear. I generally just use my hands.

#302

I applied for a job at a local restaurant. I told them I could really bring a lot to the table.

#303

Why should you buy socks with holes in them? It's the only way to get your feet in.

#304

What musical instrument is found in the bathroom? A tuba toothpaste.

#305

What country's capital is growing the fastest? Ireland. Every day it's Dublin.

#306
The CEO of Ikea was elected President of Sweden this week. He's still assembling his cabinet.

#307
My landlord told me he wanted to talk about the heating bill. I said "Sure, my door is always open."

#308
A guy walks into a bar, he was then disqualified from the limbo contest.

#309
What do you call birds that stick together? Vel-crows.

#310
I got so excited about gardening I wet my plants.

#311
Did you hear about the man who fell into an upholstery machine? He's fully recovered.

#312
How do cows keep up with current affairs? They read the Moo-spaper.

#313
Time flies like an arrow. Fruit flies like a banana.

#314
How can you tell an alligator from a crocodile? By asking if the animal will see you later, or in a while.

#315
We were so poor as kids all we had to eat was cake. Life was tough in the gateau

#316
I slept like a log. Woke up in the fireplace!

#317
At what point does a joke become a Dad joke? When it becomes apparent.

#318
What is the best way to communicate with a fish? Drop it a line.

#319
Did you hear the story about the claustrophobic astronaut? He just needed some space.

#320
What do sprinters eat before a race? Nothing, they fast!

#321

The shovel was a ground-breaking invention.

#322

What did zero say to eight? Oh wow, that belt looks great on you.

#323

How does a duck buy lipstick? She just puts it on her bill.

#324

So it turns out I'm colorblind. The news came out of the purple!

#325

Which rock group has four men that don't sing? Mount Rushmore.

#326
The Police just arrested the worlds tongue twister champion. They say he'll be given a tough sentence.

#327
I pulled a wooden shoe out my toilet today. It was clogged.

#328
When you die do you know the last part of your body to shut down? It's your pupils, they dilate.

#329
I had a dream I was floating in a sea of orange soda. It was more of a fanta sea.

#330
What's the difference between an African elephant and an Indian elephant? About 5,000 miles.

#331
What do you call a blind dinosaur? Do-you-think-he-saw-us.

#332
I went to the store to pick up 8 cans of Sprite. But when I got home I realized I'd only picked 7up.

#333
I have a joke about inferiority complexes, but it's not very good.

#334
My wife wanted me to stop acting like a flamingo. I had to put my foot down!

#335
Me and my wife have decided not to have kids. The kids are taking it pretty badly.

#336
Looks like we're out of pasta, we're penneless.

#337
How do moths swim? Butterfly stroke

#338
What do you get from a pampered cow? Spoiled milk.

#339
I wasn't going to get a brain transplant. But then I changed my mind.

#340

Why should you never use "beef stew" as a password? It's not stroganoff.

#341

Did you hear about the hungry clock? It went back four seconds.

#342

Why was the big cat disqualified from the race? Because it was a cheetah!

#343

I'm starting a new dating service in Prague. Im calling it Czech-Mate.

#344

I couldn't get a reservation at the library. They were completely booked.

#345
What does a baby PC call his father? Da-ta

#346
A year ago I had a neck brace fitted, I've never looked back since.

#347
I'd avoid the sushi if I were you. It's a little fishy!

#348
Did you hear about the cartoonist found dead at his home? Details are sketchy.

#349
I'm going to sell my vacuum cleaner, it's just gathering dust!

#350

How do you make squirrels like you?
Act like a nut.

#351

Where do cows go for
entertainment? To the movies.

#352

Why do melons have weddings?
Because they cantaloupe!

#353

I don't buy pre-shredded cheese.
Because doing it yourself is grate

#354

What do you give a pig when it's
poorly? An oink-ment!

#355
Have you heard about the record player made of chocolate? It sounds pretty sweet.

#356
As a kid my brothers used to put me in a tire and roll me down a hill. They were Goodyears!

#357
Why are cats bad storytellers? Because they only have one tale.

#358
I sometimes talk to myself when I just need expert advice.

#359
Why does Snoop Dogg always carry an umbrella? Fo' Drizzle.

#360
What do get if you make a shoe out of a banana? A slipper!

#361
In 2019 I decided not to run a marathon. I also didn't do one in 2020, 2021, or 2022. This is a running joke.

#362
What rhymes with shoe and stinks? You!

#363
A man ran into his doctor, "You've got to help me I'm shrinking." "Calm down," the doctor said. "You'll just have to learn to be a little patient."

#364
I have a joke about the flu, but I hope you don't get it.

#365
What do sea monsters eat for lunch? Fish and ships

#366
What do you call Batman when he's hurt? Bruised Wayne.

#367
Did you hear about the Pig that lost his voice? He was disgruntled

#368
Why did the scarecrow win an award? Because he was outstanding in his field.

#369

I remember the first time I saw a universal remote control. I thought to myself "well this changes everything".

#370

A woman is on trial for beating her husband with his guitar collection. The judge asked, "First offender?" She said, "No, first a Gibson! Then a Fender!"

#371

I have a rubbish job crushing cans all day. It's soda pressing.

#372

What looks like half an apple? The other half.

#373

I thought bakers would be richer.
They make so much dough.

#374

Two cannibals are eating a clown.
One says to the other: "Does this
taste funny to you?"

#375

What breed of dog can jump higher
than a skyscraper? Any breed of
dog. Skyscrapers can't jump.

#376

Why are stadiums so hot after the
game? Because all the fans have
left.

#377

I have a joke about immortality, and
it never gets old.

#378
Why do fish live in salt water?
Because pepper makes them sneeze.

#379
Do you want to hear a joke about
toilet paper? Never mind. It's
tearable.

#380
What do you call a fish with no
eyes? A fsh.

#381
What do robots eat? Computer
chips.

#382
I dropped my pillow on the floor. I
think it has a concushion.

#383

I'm cold. Then go sit in the corner it's 90 degrees!

#384

What do you call a fake noodle? An impasta.

#385

What do you get if you drive over a strawberry? Traffic jam.

#386

What do you call a magic dog? A Labracadabrador.

#387

What do you call someone who refuses to fart in public? A private tutor.

#388

The first french fries weren't cooked in France? They were cooked in Greece.

#389

Yesterday I accidentally swallowed some food colouring. The doctor says I'm ok, but I feel like I've dyed a little inside.

#390

What do you call a dinosaur that is sleeping? A dino-snore!

#391

What do you call a takeaway that gets up in your face? Too close for comfort food!

#392
What happens when you go to the bathroom in France? European.

#393
A witch's vehicle goes brrroom brrroom!

#394
I went to a seafood disco last week! Pulled a mussel!

#395
I accidentally got rice in my headphone jack. Now all my music sounds grainy.

#396
What is the least spoken language in the world? Sign language.

#397
Why do nurses like red crayons?
Sometimes they have to draw blood.

#398
Why was the belt sent to jail? For
holding up a pair of pants!

#399
I invented a car that runs on herbs.
I think I just invented thyme travel.

#400
Dad, can you make me a sandwich?
Poof! You're a sandwich.

#401
If you see a crime at an Apple
Store, are you an iWitness?

#402

Why couldn't the astronaut go to the moon? Because it was full.

#403

What do you call a cow during an earthquake? A milkshake.

#404

I used to be addicted to the hokey pokey, but I turned myself around.

#405

Learning how to collect trash wasn't hard. I just picked it up as I went along.

#406

I just watched a video where a beautiful policewoman demonstrated the use of non-lethal weapons. She was stunning!

#407
Which insect smells the best? A deodor-ant.

#408
How do you make an egg roll? Just give it a little push.

#409
What do you call a pig that does karate? A pork chop!

#410
Did you hear there was a fire at the circus? It was in tents.

#411
A magician was walking down the street, then he turned into a store.

#412

My wife laughed at me when I told her I could make a car out of macaroni. You should've seen her face when I drove pasta.

#413

It winds me up when people say age is only a number. It's clearly a word.

#414

Being an organ donor takes real guts!

#415

I needed a password eight characters long, so I picked Snow White and the Seven Dwarfs.

#416

What's blue and doesn't weigh very much? Light blue.

#417
I Just a adopted a dog from the local blacksmith, soon as I got him home he made a bolt for the door

#418
If an English teacher is convicted of a crime and doesn't complete their sentence, is that a fragment?

#419
Did you hear about the guy who invented the knock-knock joke? He won the 'no-bell' prize.

#420
What did the fish say when he hit the wall? Dam.

#421
I got a compliment on my parking today! Someone left a note on my windshield that said "parking fine."

#422
My friend said, "cheer up, it could be worse, you could be stuck underground in a hole full of water." I know he means well.

#423
How does a boar sign its name? With a pig pen.

#424
What do lazy farmers grow? Couch potatoes!

#425
How do you handle a fear of elevators? You take steps to avoid them.

#426
I have a joke about kites, but it would just sail over your head.

#427
The detectives knew what the murder weapon was instantly. It was a brief case.

#428
Do you think glass coffins will be a success? Remains to be seen.

#429
I had a dream that I was a muffler last night. I woke up exhausted!

#430

Why do cows have bells? Because their horns don't work.

#431

Can one bird make a pun? No, but toucan.

#432

Where do horses live? In neigh-borhoods.

#433

Did you hear about the guy who had his left side cut off? He's all right now!

#434

I was just thinking about my old herb garden. Good thymes.

#435

Which bear is the most condescending? A pan-duh.

#436

Dad, can you put the cat out? Why, is it on fire?

#437

How well did I hang up that picture? I nailed it.

#438

I taught a hen to count her own eggs. She's a real mathamachicken!

#439

Why do pancakes always win at baseball? They have the best batter.

#440
It's raining cats and dogs, so be careful not to step in a poodle.

#441
You must of heard about those new corduroy pillows? They're making headlines.

#442
What's green and has 5 wheels? Grass. I lied about the wheels.

#443
Why are spiders so smart? They can find everything on the web.

#444
What sort of room has no windows or doors? A mushroom!

#445

Why was the robot so tired after his road trip? He had a hard drive.

#446

I spent ages childproofing my house, but the kids still get in.

#447

During my calculus test, I was sat between two identical twins. It was hard to differentiate between them.

#448

I heard there is a new shop called Moderation. They have everything in there.

#449

What lies at the bottom of the ocean and twitches? A nervous wreck.

#450

I couldn't quite remember how to throw a boomerang. Eventually, it came back to me.

#451

What's the most remarkable invention of the last 100 years? The dry erase board

#452

Why can't you hear a Pterodactyl having a wee? Because the 'P' is silent.

#453

I can cut down a tree only using my vision. I saw it with my own eyes.

#454
I had to break up with my mathematician girlfriend. She was obsessed with an X.

#455
I wondered why the frisbee kept getting bigger and bigger. Then it hit me.

#456
How do you ask Dwayne Johnson to buy a paper cutting tool? Rock pay-for scissors.

#457
How does Moses make coffee? Hebrews it.

#458

I bought a thesaurus, and when I opened it, all the pages were blank. I can't find the words to describe how angry I am.

#459

I went to a wedding that was so beautiful, even the cake was in tiers.

#460

I read a book about anti-gravity. I couldn't put it down!

#461

An ATM got addicted to money? It suffered from withdrawals.

#462

What type of shoes do ninjas wear? Sneakers!

#463

Without geometry life is pointless.

#464

Why did the broom decide to go to bed? It was very sweepy.

#465

What's the king of all school supplies? The ruler.

#466

What do you call a pony with a sore throat? A little hoarse.

#467

I have a joke about hunting for fossils, but you probably wouldn't dig it.

#468

The furniture store keeps calling me. All I wanted was one night stand.

#469

Policeman knocks on the door, "sir it looks like your wife's been involved in an accident" man replies "I know but she has a lovely personality"

#470

What do you give a sick lemon? Lemon-aid.

#471

Why couldn't the pepper practice archery? Because it didn't habanero.

#472
What do Alexander the Great and Winnie the Pooh have in common? Their middle name.

#473
I was washing the car with my son, and he kept saying "Dad, can't you just use a sponge?"

#474
Why can't Math grow up and solve its own problems.

#475
Why shouldn't you eat a clock? It's very time-consuming.

#476
A massive shout out to my fingers. I can count on all of them

#477

Why do Swedish warships have barcodes on them? So when they dock they can Scandinavian.

#478

Why did the coach go to the bank? To get his quarter back.

#479

It's a shame about the Italian chef who died? He pasta way!

#480

Why did the Invisible Man turn down a job offer? He couldn't see himself doing it.

#481

How do you make a bouncy water bed? Add spring water.

#482

What's the difference between a man in a suit on a unicycle and a man in a tracksuit on a bicycle? Attire.

#483

What do you call a fish wearing a bowtie? Sofishticated.

#484

Why did the pirate walk the plank? His dog was back on land.

#485

Did you hear Apple might start selling its own cars, the only problem is they won't have windows.

#486

What's a tornado's favorite game? Twister!

#487
What did the janitor say when he jumped out of the closet? "Supplies!"

#488
Why shouldn't you brush your teeth with your left hand? Because a toothbrush works better.

#489
What's the best way to watch a fishing tournament? Live stream.

#490
My wife left me because I'm obsessed with pasta. I'm feeling cannelloni right now.

#491
My Dad named his dogs Rolex and Timex. They're his watch dogs!

#492

Did you hear about the square that got into a car accident? Now he's a rect-angle!

#493

Just quit my job at the Helium factory. I won't be spoken to in that tone!

#494

Every time I take my dog to the pond the ducks keep attacking him. I think is because he's pure bread.

#495

6:30 is hands down the best time on the clock.

#496

What do you get when you cross a cactus and a pig? A porky pine.

#497

Did you hear about the giant that threw up? It's all over town!

#498

I've got a joke about pizza, but it's a bit cheesy.

#499

I'm thinking about removing my spine. I feel like it's only holding me back.

#500

I'm very pleased with my new fridge magnet. So far I've got twelve fridges.

#501

Have you heard of a music group called Cellophane? They mainly wrap.

#502
How do you row a canoe filled with puppies? With a doggy paddle.

#503
My boss told me to have a good day, so I went home!

#504
How do trees access the internet? They log in.

Congratulations, you have officially graduated Dad Joke School! Now go out into the world and make everyone sigh!

If you have enjoyed this book of Dad jokes please leave a nice review on Amazon 😊

I would also love to hear any jokes you think should be included in future editions!

I also have a range of parenting books and guides available on Amazon which you can find by searching John Nero or visiting my website www.johnnero.com

SCAN ME

Printed in Great Britain
by Amazon

34302501R00066